The How to Handle
WORRY
WORKBOOK

A Catholic Approach

Praying your way through anxiety

Marshall J. Cook

D1596255

Pauline
BOOKS & MEDIA
Boston

Library of Congress Cataloging-in-Publication Data

Cook, Marshall, 1944–

The how to handle worry workbook : a Catholic approach / Marshall Cook.

    p. cm.

  ISBN 0-8198-3391-6 (pbk.)

  1. Christian life—Catholic authors. 2. Worry—Religious aspects—Catholic Church. 3. Peace of mind—Religious aspects—Catholic Church. I. Title.

  BX2350.3.C6644 2007

  248.8'6—dc22

                          2007014268

Cover design by Rosana Usselmann

Cover photo © istockphoto.com/Peter Zelei

Published by Pauline Books & Media, 50 Saint Paul's Avenue, Boston, MA 02130-3491. www.pauline.org.

Printed in the U.S.A.

Pauline Books & Media is the publishing house of the Daughters of St. Paul, an international congregation of women religious serving the Church with the communications media.

1 2 3 4 5 6 7 8 9   11 10 09 08 07

Contents

Introduction

"For God all things are possible." (Mk 10:27)

*Y*ou've probably turned to this workbook and the little text it accompanies, *How to Handle Worry: A Catholic Approach*, because you're tired of struggling with anxiety, frustration, and fatigue. If you've been suffering for a long time, change may seem impossible.

By yourself it would be. But with God, all things are possible. Use this book as a guide as you surrender yourself—including all those worries—more fully to God. The work you do here in learning to manage and master your worries can be an important part of your faith journey, trusting in God every step of the way.

You make many decisions each day—what and when you eat, how you approach and organize your work, how you spend your time away from work. What once may have been a conscious choice often becomes a habit. The journal you create on these pages will help you make those daily decisions consciously, so that they conform more completely to God's will for you.

Habits are hard to break. To convince yourself of that fact, try crossing your arms the "wrong" way, that is, with the arm that usually goes under on top. It's hard to do, isn't it? It feels strange, uncomfortable, wrong. The compulsion to re-cross your arms the "right" way, the habitual way, is very strong.

Because it's so difficult and feels unnatural, breaking habits is stressful. In trying to relieve the level of stress in your life for the long term, you're going to have to increase it for the short term.

That's where this book comes in. Let it guide you in reflecting on and evaluating the way you live and help you commit to new behaviors where appropriate. The job will require effort and commitment; the results will be more than worth it.

Here are five keys for making sure that the effort and commitment required of you in this workbook will produce positive changes in your life.

One: Write freely

The exercises in this workbook involve doing some writing. Don't worry—the goal isn't polished prose. The "Worry Journal" you create here is for your eyes only, to help you discover and explore your faith and your feelings, and to make meaningful changes in your life.

To make each writing session useful, write freely, without suppressing or judging your thoughts and without evaluating your words. I call this my "New York City cab driver's rules for free writing": don't stop and don't think. Keep pencil, pen, or keyboard fingers moving, and try not to censor or edit as you write.

Two: Enter the "timeless zone"

When you write, remove yourself from clocks and watches. Cover up the little clock on your computer screen. Set the kitchen timer or some other external device in another room where you can't see it so that you can write without constantly reminding yourself of the passing of time.

Awareness of time is one form of awareness of self. During these exercises, you need to escape your ego and explore your authentic beliefs, motivations, and fears.

Three: Do it your way

Each exercise in this workbook comes with specific instructions. Follow them—but do it your way. Adapt each session so that it speaks to your life and your needs. There is no "right" way; there is only *your* way.

Four: Give it a twenty-one day trial

In general, it takes about three weeks to erase a habit pattern and replace it with another. Try any new behavior for twenty-one days before you evaluate whether it's working for you. In other words, for the first twenty-one days, just do it. Then decide whether you should continue to do it or not.

Five: Pray without ceasing

Begin and end each session with prayer. Whenever you think about what you're doing during the day—and breaking old habits will make you very self-conscious—pray for guidance and insight.

Praise God and thank him for your life and for his overwhelming love for you. Ask for help in this and in all things. Promise to seek and follow God's will for you. He will guide you.

A brief note about the author

God will be our guide on this journey. But since I wrote the book, you deserve to know a little about what qualifies me to do so.

You can start with a lifelong tendency to worry, which I come by naturally from my mother. As my faith matured, I struggled to reconcile this contradiction: I truly believe that God loves and protects me, and yet I still suffer high anxiety at times and have trouble sleeping.

I won't say that I'm done with that process of reconciling these two realities, but I sure sleep better, and I have become fairly adept at handling the anxiety that persists.

I teach for the University of Wisconsin-Madison Division of Continuing Studies and have traveled the country, sharing what I've learned in workshops and lectures on stress and time management. (The two are entwined; it's hard to have one without the other.)

I've written several books on the subject, including the companion piece to this workbook, *How to Handle Worry: A Catholic Approach*.

I've even been on *Oprah*, where I was supposed to relieve the stress of the self-proclaimed "six worst drivers in Chicago." I don't think anybody gets "cured" in that sort of format, but I had a wonderful exchange with the good folks.

But don't place your trust in me. Pray for God's guidance and he will light your way and mine as we walk this path together.

If you're ready, let's get started.

CHAPTER 1

Bringing Your Burdens to God

"Do not fear, only believe." (Mk 5:36)

As a beginning step in handling your anxieties, keep a "Worry record" (see page 6) for three weeks. In it, note the events that make you anxious each day.

By keeping a "Worry record," you'll become much more aware of your stress responses, which will help you to know when to employ the de-stressors we'll discuss later. Eventually, you may even be able to cut off the stress response before it occurs.

You may discover some surprises. Dealing with colleagues in the workplace may be a lot more stressful for you than you thought. Others might relax and enjoy a good card game with friends, but you may find that "playing" ties you in knots you can't untangle for hours. Instead of being a reward for the week's work, having dinner guests on Friday night might be an assault on your sense of mental and emotional well-being. Cleaning the house may be as relaxing for you as a visit to a spa is for someone else, someone who hates housework.

Having a "different" response doesn't make you strange or wrong. It is simply part of what makes you who you are. To know and accept yourself is to begin to control the level of stress in your life.

Worry record

(Each day record the date, event, and how your stress was manifested.)

Week 1

~ Monday _____

_____

_____

_____

_____

~ Tuesday _____

_____

∼ Wednesday

∼ Thursday

∼ Friday

∼ Saturday _____

_____

_____

_____

_____

∼ Sunday _____

_____

_____

_____

_____

Week 2

∼ Monday _____

_____

_____

_____

_____

∼ Tuesday _____

_____

~ Wednesday

~ Thursday

~ Friday

∼ Saturday _____

_____

_____

_____

_____

∼ Sunday _____

_____

_____

_____

_____

Week 3

∼ Monday _____

_____

_____

_____

_____

∼ Tuesday _____

_____

～ Wednesday

～ Thursday

～ Friday

~ Saturday _____

_____

_____

_____

_____

_____

~ Sunday _____

_____

_____

_____

_____

Why Worry Is Inevitable

"It is I; do not be afraid." (Mt 14:27)

*W*rite a list of seven times in your life when you felt relatively carefree. Take fifteen to twenty minutes to brainstorm your list, noting everything that occurs to you, even if you aren't really sure it belongs. Note where you were, how old you were, and how long this carefree episode or stage lasted.

Eliminate distractions and interruptions while you work, and set a timer so you won't have to watch the clock. Try to keep your fingers moving on the keyboard or your writing instrument moving across the page. The important thing is not to suppress any idea that comes to you.

When you're done, set the list aside without rereading it.

The "carefree" times of my life

(Record age, place, activity / event, and duration.)

1) _____
_____
_____
_____
_____

2) _____
_____
_____
_____
_____

3) _____
_____
_____
_____
_____

4)

5)

6)

7)

Let your list "settle" for several days before revisiting it. After reading over what you wrote, strike any items that don't belong. Of those that remain (and I hope there are several), select one. It doesn't have to be the least stressful time of your life; it might be an episode or stage that is most vivid or the one you'd most enjoy reliving.

Spend about thirty minutes writing about that time. Where were you? What were you doing? Try to recall specific sensory details. What did your world look, sound, and feel like? Relax and let yourself experience that world again now.

_____

_____

_____

_____

_____

_____

_____

_____

_____

_____

_____

_____

A Time when I was relatively free of stress

Again, put your reflection aside for a day or two before reading it. When you do pick it up again, savor the experience rather than critiquing or editing the writing. Then spend as much time as you need answering these two questions:

1)   What prevents me from recapturing this experience?

Your answers may seem obvious: "I'm not four years old anymore." "I have a husband and children to take care of." "I have to earn a living." That's fine. Go ahead and write them down.

_____

_____

_____

_____

_____

_____

_____

_____

_____

_____

_____

_____

_____

2) What elements from that time can I recreate in my life today?

By writing about a relatively carefree time in your life, you've created a waking daydream. You may be able to bring a little bit of that fantasy into your "real" life. Is there anything about that time and place that you can incorporate into your life now? Spend as much time as you need on this question.

_____

_____

_____

_____

_____

_____

_____

_____

_____

_____

_____

_____

_____

_____

_____

_____

_____

CHAPTER 3

Christmas Comes but Once a Year—Thank God!

"Martha, Martha, you worried and distracted by many things;
there is need of only one thing." (Lk 10:41–42)

The Christmas season can be an especially stressful time—and provides an excellent opportunity to try another de-stressor. During the "holidays," most of us work much harder than usual, trying to keep up with family and work obligations while somehow shopping, planning, and partying. And we're supposed to be gloriously happy while we do it—an added source of stress.

There's just too much activity to fit into the available time. To deal with this sort of stress, we need to apply a proven technique of time management. The real goal of time management should be to help you put your time where your values are, instead of where the most urgent-seeming demands are.

Adapting a technique first described by Stephen Covey in his breakthrough book *The 7 Habits of Highly Effective People*, you'll sort activities into four levels. You'll consider the urgency of the activity—the amount of time pressure you feel in completing it—as well as its relative *value* to you.

Level 1: The activity carries a great sense of urgency and is of great value.

Level 2: The activity carries a great sense of urgency but is of lesser value.

Level 3: The activity carries little sense of urgency but is of great value.

Level 4: The activity seems neither especially urgent nor valuable.

An *urgent* activity requires action quickly or by a certain deadline. A valuable activity pertains directly to the most important elements in your life, things like faith and family. An activity may provide great intrinsic or extrinsic rewards but it still may not relate to your core values.

I find *Level 1* activities the easiest to define. When I learned that my father was in the last stages of his journey through cancer, for example, I dropped everything, threw the to-do list out the window, and flew to California to be with him. God gave me the difficult and rich blessing of spending the last week of my father's life with him.

I didn't have to do any time managing on that occasion. Level 1 activities take precedence over everything else. I did do a little worrying, however—about how my little world in Madison, Wisconsin, could possibly function without me while I was gone. Turns out it functioned just fine. Problems got solved, went away, or were waiting for me when I got back. Western civilization showed no signs of crumbling.

Level 2 is a bit trickier. A phone call, voice or e-mail, or a yell down the hall summons you to a meeting. "It's starting right now!" you're told. The summons is urgent, but before you start running, consider whether or not this particular meeting is important—or if it's important that you be there.

That meeting—and many of our daily tasks, including a high percentage of phone calls and e-mails—may fall into the *Level 2* category.

Level 3 is also tricky. Just about everybody now agrees that good diet and regular rest and exercise are important to maintain good health, for example. Most of us consider good health to be a core value or at least a very good thing. But the notion of exercising right now may not seem urgent.

Exercise, financial planning, even nourishing personal relationships may fall into this category—and may thus be neglected.

That brings us to *Level 4*, the goofing-off category. I work (play?) the *New York Times* crossword puzzle just about every day, for example. Urgent? Surely not. Of great importance? Not really. I do the puzzles because I like them. It's just plain fun for a word nerd like me.

Should I cut them out because they're neither urgent nor important? Well, yeah, on the busy days, I can cut out the crossword puzzle and watching that second local newscast and reading the baseball box scores. But on days when things cool to the normal slow boil, I'll do these things because I enjoy them. I want to be efficient, but I don't want life to seem like one long root canal procedure.

Over the next few days, list your daily activities and try to fit each into one of these four categories:

Level 1

_____

_____

_____

_____

_____

_____

_____

Level 2

_____

_____

_____

_____

_____

_____

_____

Level 3

Level 4

After several days of collecting and reflecting, you should have a pretty good list for each level. Once you've got raw materials to work with, you're ready to do some true values-based time management.

Your goal is to shift some of your time each day out of *Level 2* and into *Level 3* by scheduling time for the activities that mean the most but currently get the least attention. This will take time, effort, dedication, and strong motivation, but no other aspect of time management pays bigger dividends.

For now, hang onto these lists. When you get to Chapter 6, you'll use them to make conscious choices about how you spend your time.

You'll want to revisit this exercise any time you become especially busy and most highly stressed—when a daughter gets married, for example, or when you change jobs. It's an especially useful tool during the Thanksgiving, Christmas, New Year holiday season. Consider taking time a few weeks before Thanksgiving for some values-based time management.

CHAPTER 4

Why Worry Hurts Us

*"Can any of you by worrying add a single hour
to your span of life?" (Mt 6:27)*

As you learn to monitor the amount of stress you're feeling, you can also begin to differentiate between "good stress" and "bad stress," anticipation and anxiety. You can then work to attain "eustress"—the ideal level of tension in your life.

Your goal won't be to eliminate all stress from your life. You couldn't even if you tried, and you wouldn't like it if you did. Life involves stress, whether you live alone, in an unstable relationship, or even in a stable one; whether you're your own boss, work for an ogre, or don't have a paying job at all; whether you live in city, town, or country.

Another word for "good stress" is "motivation." Good stress gets us out of bed in the morning and prepares us to tackle the day's challenges. It sharpens focus, releases energy, and gives life meaning and purpose. Raising children, nurturing relationships, and performing work for the greater glory of God all provide this sort of good stress. But the same stressors that create good energy can also trigger crippling anxiety.

What's the difference? How you perceive a challenge and whether you freely choose to accept it play a role. The level of stress you're comfortable with also helps determine how you react. Often, it's simply a matter of degree: too many good stressors can become unmanageable, anxiety-producing "bad stress."

Achieving eustress, then, involves eliminating bad stress when possible and making sure that the amount of good stress doesn't become overwhelming.

For the next week, as you continue to note the stressors in your life, try dividing them into two piles: "good stress" and "bad stress."

On the "good" list go activities that create some tension for you but that you genuinely enjoy and profit from. You're willing to continue to pay the price in stress for the results you achieve.

The "bad" list includes activities that create an inappropriately high level of anxiety or that simply aren't worth the tension they produce. You pay too high a price, and you don't get enough reward in return.

Don't be concerned at this point with trying to eliminate the "bad" activities (which may, indeed, be impossible to do in many cases). You're working toward increased awareness. Coping strategies come later.

Prepare your lists of good and bad stressors. Initially, spend perhaps ten to fifteen minutes and come back to the list three or four times throughout the week until you're satisfied that the lists are thorough and accurate.

"*Good Stress*"   "*Bad Stress*"

_____   _____
_____   _____
_____   _____
_____   _____
_____   _____
_____   _____
_____   _____
_____   _____
_____   _____
_____   _____
_____   _____
_____   _____
_____   _____
_____   _____
_____   _____
_____   _____
_____   _____
_____   _____

Chapter 5

Faith Healing and Positive Thinking

"Do not worry about anything, but in everything by prayer and supplication with thanksgiving let your requests be made known to God." (Phil 4:6)

North Americans pride themselves on being an optimistic, "can-do" people, and some of us put a great deal of stock in the power of a positive attitude to successfully meet life's challenges.

Our Catholic faith exhorts us to put our trust in God, to turn our troubles over to the Lord, and to trust that, ultimately, "all will be well, all will be well, and all manner of things will be well" (Julian of Norwich).

In this exercise in self-awareness, you'll keep a prayer log for a week, trying to determine your expectations for prayer and God's expectations and desires for you.

Look closely at your relationship with God and how this relationship is expressed in your prayer. Note ritual prayers such as the Rosary, grace at meals, and the Mass. Also record your own personal prayers, including any petitions you make spontaneously. You'll have to decide whether a muttered, "Oh, God, please get me to my doctor's appointment on time!" actually constitutes a prayer directed to God or is simply a vocalized expression of desire and need that happens to have God's name in it.

The point here is not to determine whether you're praying enough or the right kind of prayer. If you later decide that the quantity and/or quality of your prayer needs adjusting, so be it. But this exercise aims at a realization of your true expectations when you pray and of your relationship with God.

Ritual scheduled prayers   *Spontaneous prayers*

_____   _____

_____   _____

_____   _____

_____   _____

_____   _____

_____   _____

_____   _____

_____   _____

Ritual scheduled prayers   *Spontaneous prayers*

_____   _____

_____   _____

_____   _____

_____   _____

_____   _____

_____   _____

_____   _____

_____   _____

_____   _____

_____   _____

_____   _____

_____   _____

When you have finished your weeklong journal, put it away for a day or two. Then go back over it. See if anything you've written strikes you as unexpected or unusual. Write a brief journal entry answering the following two questions about your prayer life: *"When I pray, what do I expect to happen?"* and *"When I pray, what is my experience of God?"*

An honest answer to these questions can reveal a great deal about your prayer expectations and perhaps even something about God's expectations for you.

"What do I expect to happen?"

_____

_____

_____

_____

_____

_____

_____

"What is my experience of God?"

_____

_____

_____

_____

_____

_____

_____

CHAPTER 6

Why Time Management Couldn't Save Us from Ourselves

"Do not be afraid, little flock, for it is your Father's good pleasure to give you the kingdom." (Lk 12:32)

"There just aren't enough hours in the day." Despite all the gadgets that are supposed to help us get more done in less time, we seem to be perpetually hurrying from one task to the next, with barely enough time to breathe.

That kind of hurry produces stress and may provoke anxiety.

Since God isn't making any more hours in a day, to manage stress, you'll need to manage time.

You can't "save time," "borrow time," "have time," or even "waste time." You can only live; time is one way you measure your life.

No one will ever give you time, and you'll never find time. It isn't lost. You're living it, every moment of your life.

If you want to have time to do something you're not now doing, and if your day already seems full to bursting, then you have to *make time*—which is to say, you have to take time from an established activity to give to the new one. It's a trade.

If you want to schedule half an hour of exercise every morning before you shower and go to work, you have to figure out what thirty-minute activity you won't do that you normally would do that day. Make your time equation balance.

As with any budget (and time management is, after all, nothing more or less than a budget for time), you can make things seem to balance on paper without really changing the reality. To create your half hour for exercise, for example, you could decide to give up thirty minutes of leisure reading after dinner. Your trade looks fine on paper, but if you aren't actually taking that thirty minutes for leisure reading after dinner, you're going to come up half an hour short at the end of the day.

Make the trade intentionally and consciously. If you don't, one of two things will happen, both bad:

1) You'll soon quit the half hour of exercise, deciding you just don't "have" the time, or

2) By default, you'll take the thirty minutes from elsewhere, most likely either sleep or relationships.

Whatever choice you make, make it consciously.

Let's try a little exercise in time management. Any trade you make in this exercise will be hypothetical. You could make the trade if you decided to. It will remain hypothetical until and unless you actually act on it and integrate the new activity into your life.

In the left-hand column, note an activity you want or need to be doing that you're having trouble "finding" the time for now. (You'll probably find these activities on the Level Three list you made in Chapter 3.) In the right-hand column, list the possible trades you might make to create the needed time.

For example, suppose you decide to start praying the Rosary daily before work as a way to deepen and strengthen your spiritual life. You estimate that saying a Rosary will take you about ten minutes. (Don't underestimate to "make the books balance"; you'll only be fooling yourself. Let's give the Rosary fifteen minutes.)

List this desired new activity in the left column and then brainstorm the places where those fifteen minutes might come from. For example:

New activity:	*Old activity:*
Say the Rosary daily (15 minutes)	Don't read the morning paper.
	Get up 15 minutes earlier.
	Skip breakfast.
	Take 15 minutes for lunch instead of 30.
	Demand that your husband wash the dinner dishes.
	Spend 45 minutes instead of the usual hour reading magazines.
	Stop watching *Entertainment Tonight* (which would actually liberate 30 minutes!).

Perhaps none of those options sounds especially good. You can make perfectly sound arguments for maintaining all of these activities. You need to be informed, you need your rest, breakfast is the most important meal of the day, and you shouldn't gulp down lunch and rush back to work.

There just doesn't seem to be any fat to cut from your schedule. Now brainstorm some more.

New activity

Old activity

New activity

Old activity

Put the list aside and come back to it fresh in a day or so. See if your subconscious has come up with any other possible trades.

If you decide to implement a trade, make your decision and write it down, with a *specific* start-up date and *specific* time of day.

"Starting next Monday, I will pray the Rosary from 6:30 to 6:45 P.M. every weekday. I will give up watching the first half of Entertainment Tonight *to balance the equation."*

You've made your decision. Now stick with it. Keep your Monday promise—and continue to live out your trade for at least four weeks! (That's twenty weekdays of praying the Rosary. Remember, it takes about twenty days to begin to establish a new habit pattern.)

After your initial trial run, reevaluate your decision and see if it's working for you.

Suppose that, instead of making a trade, you wrote the following statement:

"I'm not willing to trade any available activity to pray the Rosary. It was a nice idea, but it isn't going to work out."

What possible good could that do?

It certainly won't get the Rosary prayed. But it will mean that you're living intentionally, and you don't have to fret and re-decide every time it occurs to you that you "ought" to be praying the Rosary. You've made that decision.

It would also make an honest person out of you. You can no longer tell yourself, "I don't have time to pray the Rosary." You'll have to say, instead, "I have chosen to live my time in another way."

There's real power in that.

CHAPTER 7

Casting Out Demons and Unclean Spirits

*"What sort of man is this, that even
the winds and the sea obey him?" (Mt 8:27)*

Jesus had power over nature, including the ability to calm our
inner as well as outer storms. He conferred the ability to cast
out demons on his disciples, thus establishing the biblical founda-
tion for the rite of exorcism.

Modern science has names and treatments for many of the symptoms of demon possession Jesus confronted. Epilepsy triggers seizures and convulsions. Someone suffering from schizophrenia may hear voices.

By any name and in any time, such illnesses, along with manic-depression (bipolar disorder), clinical depression, obsessive compulsive disorder, and others require more than the sorts of coping mechanisms we're discussing here. Doctors diagnose and treat a variety of lesser but still serious illnesses, conditions, and syndromes, including panic disorder, posttraumatic stress disorder, and hundreds of phobias.

The line between being stressed-out and having a mental disorder isn't always clear. If you have doubts, you should see a mental health professional for diagnostic testing.

Fortunately, most of the time, environmental factors (stressors) account for our symptoms, and a few simple stress management techniques can alleviate them. We can cast out some of our own mental demons by learning to relax in the midst of our daily storms.

In this workout, you're going to focus on one of the most effective strategies for coping with normal anxiety. You're going to learn to take four vacations every day.

Then you're going to ask yourself the famous "Lakein question."

First draw up a list of potential "vacations" you could take in the midst of your most frenzied day. Imagine everything from a "found" fifteen minutes when a meeting lets out early to the twenty-seven seconds you're required to wait at a red light.

In good weather, I often eat lunch out by Lake Mendota, a two-minute walk from my office. This usually takes about fifteen minutes and provides a wonderful mini-vacation.

For another break, I'll walk the six flights of stairs down to the first floor for a cup of water or a Diet Coke from the vending machine. (My knees and hips have forced me to take the elevator back up most days, and I don't find elevators particularly restful, but the overall effect is beneficial.)

Often, I'll simply push back from my desk and treat myself to a minute of slow, luxurious stretching, gently rotating my shoulders to get the literal and figurative kinks out. A minute of this is remarkably restorative—and saves me from the knotted neck that often used to plague me by mid-afternoon.

My daily routine includes prayer—communal when I can make the daily Mass at St. Paul's near my office—reflection on the daily readings in the Missal, and silence.

I also try to get in a session or two of belly breathing. I haven't taken a class in meditative breathing. I don't count breaths. I just breathe deeply—consciously, slowly, and from the gut.

Try it right now. Slowly and deeply. Let the belly expand. Feel the restorative stream of oxygen flood your poor, parched system. Remarkable!

You can do this in the middle of a meeting, and nobody has to know. (You don't have to make huffing noises for the breathing to "work"; you just breathe!)

Sometimes I can treat myself to a bookstore browse or a twenty-minute walk by the lake. These longer breaks are bliss. But they're usually impossible to schedule. I can get by quite nicely on four mini-vacations each day.

List several vacation activities you might incorporate into your daily schedule and times when they'd be most beneficial.

Mini-vacation time

_____

_____

_____

_____

_____

_____

_____

_____

_____

_____

You're probably going to have to schedule these breaks and then remind and even force yourself to take them. For type A worriers like us, breaking the work momentum is counterintuitive. Nonstop work is one of those habit patterns that has grown to feel "right"—especially when the work is going well and you're on a roll. But when you break the momentum, you also break the stress cycle, preventing the pain of a mental cramp at the end of the day that can keep you from being able to relax and sleep.

Figure out how you're going to remind yourself to take your breaks. You can post sticky notes, program your computer to prompt you, or even set an alarm (but not a shrill, clanging one!). Let a natural daily occurrence be your prompter. From my office, for example, I can hear the long, low wail of what sounds like a ship's horn every afternoon.

You're going to have to make a conscious effort to take these breaks, and sometimes you'll forget. (Feelings of tension will remind you, but that's what you're trying to avoid.) It will take several weeks for these mini-vacations to become habit. But when they do, you'll wonder how you ever got along without them.

You'll likely get an added benefit that will amaze you. By taking a few minutes of vacation on a busy day, you'll actually find yourself getting more done in less time! There's no magic here. The breaks refresh and restore you, and you work more efficiently after having taken them.

Convince yourself by doing it.

When you take these daily pauses—and longer ones on the good days, when you're not quite so rushed—ask yourself the "Lakein question," the challenge Alan Lakein poses in his marvelous 1973 book, *Time Management: How to Get Control of Your Time and Your Life*. The wording may vary, but this is the essence:

"Is this what I want or need to be doing right now?"

The "this" in the sentence refers to whatever you're doing at the moment.

Become accustomed to asking yourself this question several times during your journey through each day. You may catch yourself taking a detour by doing a low-priority, non-urgent task simply because it's easier than the more important one you're putting off (and worrying about). You may even find yourself doing something you neither want nor need to do at all!

If this happens, make a midcourse adjustment so you'll get to your destination safely, on time, and relaxed. This is grassroots time management at it's finest!

For the first week or so, keep a journal, noting the time and place and what you were doing when you asked yourself the Lakein question. Briefly note how you reacted to the question. This will help you remember to ask the question and to see what benefit you get from answering it.

Lakein diary

(Record date, time, place, activity, and reactions.)

_____

_____

_____

_____

_____

_____

_____

_____

_____

_____

_____

_____

_____

_____

_____

_____

_____

CHAPTER 8

Don't Sweat the Small Stuff

"With the LORD on my side I do not fear.
What can mortals do to me?" (Ps 118:6)

Before you can effectively confront your worry, you need to know what you're really worried about. This may sound simpleminded and unnecessary. Hey, we're worry experts, right? We don't need any help being better worriers!

Worry thrives on vagueness. The less defined the worry, the stronger the feeling. Often, being able to state the precise worry is the first and most important step in robbing it of its power over you.

Even before you can define the worry, however, you need to catch yourself entertaining it. Most of us become quite adept at shoving our anxieties into the mental closet, ignoring them so they'll just go away. They don't, of course. They feed and grow strong in the darkness of that closet. You hear them banging on the door all day long in your subconscious, and they corrode your mental, emotional, and physical well-being.

Take mental and emotional stock during one of your daily breaks. If you hear the worry nagging, throw open that closet door and let it out into the open air. Give it specific shape and substance. Underneath the general dread of beginning that task you've been putting off all week, what are you really afraid of?

Write about what you discover. You may surprise yourself. For example, many writers I know assume that it's fear of failure that makes their stomachs knot up when they face the terror of a blank computer screen. Many discover that it's success, not failure, they fear! (*What if somebody actually publishes my stuff and people read it? I'll be exposed for the fraud I am! They'll expect me to do it again!*)

A marvelous therapist named Kathleen Levenick taught me how to "tie a string" to my anxieties by fully experiencing them and then tracing them back through my memories, recalling an earlier time when I felt the same thing. I recommend this technique to you. This journey may carry you all the way back to grade school, perhaps even earlier. You didn't just invent the anxiety, after all.

This exercise is useful in itself. It's also perfect preparation for your first "worry appointment," which you're going to schedule in the next chapter.

Specific anxiety	Earlier experience of the same anxiety

Specific anxiety

Earlier experience of
the same anxiety

_____

_____

_____

_____

_____

_____

_____

_____

_____

_____

_____

_____

_____

_____

_____

_____

_____

_____

Chapter 9

Meeting Worry Head-On

"But I call upon God, and the Lord will save me." (Ps 55:16)

Congratulations. You're now ready for your first worry appointment. Of all the exercises you do on this journey, this one may sound the strangest if you tried to explain it. If that's the case, don't bother. Don't even try to explain it to yourself. Just do it. Schedule a worry session—or call it something else if you want. Perhaps "hissy fit" or "simmering in the stew." Whatever works.

Get your day planner or calendar and mark off at least three sessions "in the stewpot" over the next week or so.

How's first thing in the morning for you? What about right after lunch? A nice mid-afternoon hissy fit? Figure out what works best for your schedule. Just make sure you plan it so that you're not doing anything else but worrying! Don't do this while you're driving, taking a walk, watching television, or even just letting the radio keep you company. Find a secluded place where you can sit comfortably and just simply worry!

Again, use an external timer (egg timer, timer on the kitchen stove, the time it takes for the coffee to perk, whatever). That way, you don't have to be consciously aware of time, and you don't have to keep checking. You can devote yourself fully to worrying. How?

This part really is easy—but it can be quite painful, even scary.

Let the worry flood over you. You've been holding it back, hiding it, refusing to look it in the eye. Now embrace it! Feel it—all of it! Sometimes when I do this, my body literally quakes with internal tremors. That's the bad news. You really have to let yourself experience the worry, teeth and all.

It's also the good news, because that's all you have to do. Just feel it. Don't fight it or try to fix it. Don't talk yourself out of it or talk back to it. Don't verify, justify, rationalize, or deny. Just feel.

Devote ten minutes to your worry. It will seem like a lot. When the timer goes off, gather yourself up and get back to your day. You may feel shaky. You may be exhausted! You'll likely be somewhat relieved, possibly even refreshed. You faced the enemy, surrendered to it, and you're still here. Life goes on. You didn't die! In fact, it probably wasn't as bad as you thought it would be.

The worry has likely gotten tired of banging on you and has gone away. But don't become complacent; it will return! You've only tired it out, not slain it. When it does return, unbidden, as you're trying to sleep or pray or think, gently banish it, reminding it that you'll give it your full and undivided attention at your next appointment. Remind it of the time and place and tell it not to be late.

This sounds silly, but it works!

Schedule your first three worry sessions right now.

Worry session

(Day, time, place, worry—if you know in advance what it will be.)

CHAPTER 10

Moving from Worrying to Doing

"The steadfast love of the LORD never ceases, his mercies never come to an end;
they are new every morning; great is your faithfulness." (Lam 3:22–23)

W ithin this chapter of *How to Handle Worry*, I identified a few
of my personal heroes, people who overcame great obsta-
cles (and the doubts and fears that must have accompanied them) to
achieve great goals. Among them are baseball star/civil rights
leader/philanthropist Roberto Clemente, and my father, Lieu-
tenant Commander George Cook. I could have listed many more

people. By studying how my heroes faced and overcame their own doubts and anxieties, I've become better able to accept and overcome my own.

Take a few minutes to list some of your own heroes (or role models or whatever term applies). Set the list aside for a few days. Add to it as other names occur to you.

Chamber of champions

_____

_____

_____

_____

_____

_____

_____

_____

_____

_____

_____

_____

_____

When you're ready, select one of your champions for closer study. Hold this person up to the Lord in prayer, thanking God for the example and the inspiration he or she has given you.

Take about thirty minutes—again, using some sort of external timer—to write a free-form biography of this person, the challenges he or she faced, so far as you know of them, and what he or she did to overcome them.

Finally, write your conclusion, the specific lesson(s) you can take from this champion's life to apply to your own.

Reflections on a champion

_____

_____

_____

_____

_____

_____

_____

_____

_____

_____

_____

_____

CHAPTER 11

Naming and Defeating Five Varieties of Worry

"Even the darkness is not dark to you; the night is as bright as the day, for darkness is as light to you." (Ps 139:12)

It's time to tackle one of your personal demons, following this six-step process detailed in *How to Handle Worry*.

Step 1: Don't resist or deny the anxiety.

Face and feel the fear. Let it wash over you, through you. (Your "worry appointment" has been good practice for this.) Stop fearing the fear. Your panic will subside. You'll feel relief, even peace. Worry will have done its worst.

Step 2: Give form to the fear.

The worst anxieties are often the least specific. I call such general, free-floating dread "the formless furies." Give your fear a name. Write it down here, in as specific terms as you can. (Not "I'm afraid of public speaking" but "I'm terrified of having to get up in front of the congregation during Mass and read the Epistle this Sunday.")

If you find it helpful, categorize the fear based on the five types outlined in Chapter 11 of *How to Handle Worry*:

- fear based on ignorance;
- fear of the future;
- fear stemming from the past;
- inertia;
- evasion.

Fear of reading at Mass is clearly fear of some challenge required of you in the future, for example.

Formless fury unmasked

_____

_____

_____

_____

_____

_____

Track the fear to its source if you can ("tie a string to it," as mentioned earlier). When was the first time you remember being anxious about speaking in front of a group? Of simply being among a group of people? (I can vaguely recall the fit I threw when my mother tried to take me to kindergarten on what was supposed to be my first day of school.)

Tracing the fear to its source

Step 3: Push the fear to the extreme.

If you haven't tried it, you may not believe it yet, but this step can be fun!

Imagine the worst-case scenario. What's the worst thing that can happen to you, for example, when you get up to read the Epistle? Be specific.

Worst-case scenario

_____

_____

_____

_____

_____

_____

_____

_____

_____

_____

_____

_____

_____

Did you live through it? Good. (Of course, that's the point.) Now estimate the odds that this worst-case scenario, or something like it, will actually occur. Finally, visualize and write out the *best-case* scene. Imagine yourself performing flawlessly, everything going perfectly. This is the movie you'll want to play and replay in your mind as you prepare for the challenge.

Best-case scenario

_____

_____

_____

_____

_____

_____

_____

_____

_____

_____

_____

_____

_____

_____

_____

_____

Step 4: Figure out what, if anything, you can do and when you can do it.

Dilemmas offer choices, even if they don't at first appear to. You may have options here, actions and non-actions you haven't considered. Spend a few minutes brainstorming on the particular anxiety you named in Step 1.

- For worry thriving on ignorance, think of ways to get the information you need.

- For worry lurking in the future, think of ways you can prepare.

- For worry festering in the past, think of what, if anything, you can do to make amends or undo the damage.

- For worry feeding on inertia, think of specific actions you can take.

- For worry thriving on evasion, think of ways you might seek guidance in confronting the task.

What you'll do and when you'll do it

_____

_____

_____

_____

_____

_____

_____

_____

_____

_____

_____

_____

_____

_____

In the case of proclaiming the Word of God at Mass, it might at first seem as if you only have two real options: do it or don't do it. (If you decide not to do it, you'll probably have to do something else: tell somebody, arrange for a substitute, buy a ticket for a Saturday flight to Thailand….)

Here are a few other things you could do:

1) Over-prepare: practice reading the piece aloud several times beyond when you think you've mastered it.

2) Read a commentary on the Epistle, so you'll truly feel you "own" and understand it.

3) Seek advice/help from someone who does a good job of proclaiming the Word. You'll probably get good tips and reassurance ("Everybody's nervous, especially the first few times"), and you'll also flatter the person you ask.

4) Tape record yourself reading and play it back for critique.

5) Or practice in front of an "audience" of your spouse, family, or friends.

Whatever you decide to do, the more you prepare, the more you'll alleviate your anxiety.

Write down specifically what you plan to do and when you plan to do it. This is your action plan. Without making it concrete in this way, all your planning will be for nothing. Refer to this plan whenever the anxiety returns.

Action plan

_____

_____

_____

_____

_____

_____

_____

_____

_____

_____

_____

_____

_____

_____

_____

_____

_____

_____

_____

Now you're ready to make a 3 x 5-inch (or 6 x 9-inch for big worriers like me) prayer card, noting:

1) your specific definition or description of the problem;

2) the action option you've selected;

3) the specific date and time you'll take the action.

Carry the card with you. Pray over it often.

Step 5: Act in spite of your fear.

When you follow through and implement your action plan, you'll begin to discover a life-changing secret:

Courage isn't lack of fear. It's action in the face of fear.

There are two pleasing corollaries to this axiom:

1) You don't look as afraid as you feel—not even close.

2) Folks are rooting for you to do well.

In the case of the Sunday morning showdown, everyone in the congregation (including the priest) can relate to nervousness about public speaking. With maybe one or two sadistic exceptions, they all want you to do well (for your sake, certainly, and because hearing the Word clearly proclaimed will uplift and instruct them).

You're playing before the home crowd.

Step 6: Abide by your decision and its consequences.

Whatever happens—and I'm betting you'll do a great job— make your decision and perform your intention with your whole heart and all your energy. Don't second-guess. If you don't get the results you want, amend or replace your decision with another one for next time.

In the immortal words of my favorite philosopher, Satchel Paige, "Don't look back. Somebody might be gaining on you."

Making a Time and Place for Prayer

"For those who want to save their life will lose it,
and those who lose their life for my sake will find it."(Mt 16:25)

*U*nfortunately, for many of us, prayer may fall into the Level 3 category. Of course you should pray. You'll feel better when you do. But not right now! You're too busy.

Spontaneous prayers probably well up in you several times a day. ("Oh, God! Please let me get there on time!" "What a beautiful sunset. Thank you, Lord!") But you can probably benefit from daily planned prayer as well.

I schedule a time, place, and form for daily prayer, and I keep that appointment as faithfully as I would one with any significant person in my life. I highly recommend the practice; it has been one of God's greatest gifts to me.

Here are a few of the forms that scheduled daily prayer can take:

- daily Mass;
- the Rosary or other vocal prayer, alone or in a group;
- simple prayers of praise, thanksgiving, contrition, and petition;
- focused, intercessory prayer, in which you hold up a person or problem to the Lord, seeking guidance and grace;
- meditation on or contemplation of a particular passage of Sacred Scripture;
- an inventory of behavior based on the Ten Commandments.

You can no doubt think of many others.

Find forms that work for you. Integrate them into your daily schedule. Then adhere to your self-prescribed pattern for at least three full weeks, twenty-one days, before trying to evaluate its effects on you.

Here is a week's worth of slots for you to turn into a prayer plan. Do one in pencil, put it aside, pray and reflect on it, and, when you're ready, ink in a schedule you're willing to try for at least twenty-one days.

Prayer calendar

(Record the time, location, and type of prayer.)

Week 1

～ Monday _____

_____

_____

～ Tuesday _____

_____

_____

～ Wednesday _____

_____

_____

～ Thursday _____

_____

_____

~ Friday _____

_____

_____

~ Saturday _____

_____

_____

~ Sunday _____

_____

_____

Week 2

≈ Monday _____

_____

_____

≈ Tuesday _____

_____

_____

≈ Wednesday _____

_____

_____

≈ Thursday _____

_____

_____

~ Friday _____

_____

_____

~ Saturday _____

_____

_____

~ Sunday _____

_____

_____

Week 3

～ Monday

_____

_____

_____

～ Tuesday

_____

_____

_____

～ Wednesday

_____

_____

_____

～ Thursday

_____

_____

_____

~ Friday _____

_____

_____

~ Saturday _____

_____

_____

~ Sunday _____

_____

_____

CHAPTER 13

Maintaining the Temple of the Spirit

"Come to me, all you that are weary and are carrying heavy burdens,
and I will give you rest." (Mt 11:28)

You don't have to exercise. For that matter, you don't have to pray, obey the Commandments, honor your marriage vows, pay your taxes, or show up for work when you're supposed to. God gives us free will, including the choice to love him and others freely or to withhold that love. But all those things are very, very good ideas.

Regular exercise provides marvelous stress relief, but there are other benefits, too. Some of these include:

- muscle tone;
- endurance;
- energy;
- weight loss and maintenance;
- appearance;
- sense of physical, mental, and emotional well-being;
- self-righteous smugness when you're done.

Okay, I probably shouldn't have listed that last one, but I'm sure I could have listed many more, and so can you.

Most people concede that exercise is important. (Most but not all. Was it Oscar Wilde who first said, "Whenever I feel the urge to exercise, I lay down until it passes"?) But alas, it often falls into that Level 3 category, at least until a doctor tells us to exercise or die.

Many are daunted by nightmarish visions of ultra-marathons and "no pain, no gain" workouts in the gym. Exercise, however, can take many forms, and moderate exercise can yield big benefits.

Forms of exercise include:

- community recreation programs (Pilates, aerobics, yoga, and many more);
- jogging;
- weightlifting;
- lap swimming;
- vigorous walking;
- biking (outdoor or stationary);
- treadmill workout.

Some of these require instruction and/or equipment, and all require discipline. If you choose this sort of exercise, it's vital to find a good fit, to start slowly, and to stick with it for at least the mandatory twenty-one-day count.

Let's brainstorm other ways to work body movement into the day. I'll start.

- Take the stairs instead of the elevator.
- Park farther away from work.
- Leave the car at home and walk or bike to work.

I especially love that last one, because it requires exercise, provides transportation, saves money, is more convenient—it's much easier to park a bike than a car in downtown Madison!—and probably does Mother Earth a tiny bit of good.

- Take the dog for a walk. (I've heard it said that if your dog's too fat, you're not getting enough exercise.)
- Go dancing.
- Play ping-pong. (No law says you can't have fun while you move.)

Now it's your turn.

Ways to incorporate movement into my day

_____

_____

_____

_____

_____

_____

_____

_____

_____

_____

_____

_____

_____

_____

_____

_____

_____

_____

_____

_____

_____

_____

_____

If you'd like to work regular exercise into your daily routine, now's the time to begin. Again, I'll provide the chart, and you make the trade-off that will create a little time to move your body.

Daily exercise calendar

(Record activity, time, location, and activity given up to make time.)

∼ Monday _____

_____

_____

_____

∼ Tuesday _____

_____

_____

_____

∼ Wednesday _____

_____

_____

_____

∼ Thursday _____

_____

_____

_____

~ Friday _____

_____

_____

_____

~ Saturday _____

_____

_____

_____

~ Sunday _____

_____

_____

_____

CHAPTER 14

Five Ways to Get Worry to Work for You

"Do not worry about tomorrow,
for tomorrow will bring worries of its own." (Mk 6:34)

On the corresponding chapter in *How to Handle Worry*, I shared my great adventure appearing on the *Oprah Winfrey Show*. I might have subtitled it: "A case study in dealing with extreme anxiety." It had all the classic elements designed to create inner turmoil:

- a new and unknown experience;
- disruption of my normal routine;
- unfamiliar surroundings;
- high stakes—I get to make an idiot out of myself in front of a few million rather than a few dozen people;
- and, as if all that weren't enough, I had to drive to Chicago and find a parking space!

I survived, and so did Oprah and the rest of civilization. Whatever I said and did—I've never looked at the tape—it doesn't seem to have left any noticcable scar tissue. I learned a lot and gained confidence.

To fully benefit from that sort of learning, spend some time on yourself here with a two-part probe into your own life experience.

First, list several anxiety-filled times in your life, specific things such as first day on the new job, first day of X-grade at Y-school, a life-altering test, your wedding day, things like that.

Life's scariest moments

_____

_____

_____

_____

_____

_____

_____

_____

_____

Now choose one of these moments and write about it in the "Anxiety memoir" below. Include how you felt beforehand, how you coped with your anxiety, what happened to the anxiety when you actually encountered the experience, and how everything worked out.

Set the writing aside for a day or more, then read it and draw whatever conclusions you think might be helpful to you in facing your next anxiety-laden challenge.

Anxiety memoir

_____

_____

_____

_____

_____

_____

_____

_____

_____

_____

_____

_____

_____

_____

Don't Get Mad. Don't Get Even. Get Peaceful.

"Beloved, never avenge yourselves...for it is written,
'Vengeance is mine, I will repay, says the Lord.'" (Rom 12:19)

Time to vent! Make a list of your pet peeves, things in daily life that anger and frustrate you. Since many of these likely involve other people, we could call it "The Roll Call of Bozos." Fire away; don't be shy. It's even okay to enjoy it.

The bozo brigade

_____

_____

_____

_____

_____

_____

_____

_____

_____

_____

_____

Don't look at the list for at least a day. When you return to it, see if you have anything more to add. When you're finished, select one pet peeve/Bozo and write a specific strategy for dealing with it/him/her in a way that will reduce your anger. The "solution" may or may not actually "solve" anything. It will likely have little or no effect on any particular Bozos involved.

The goal here is to develop strategies for reducing your own stress level.

How to relieve stress

_____

_____

_____

_____

_____

_____

_____

_____

_____

_____

_____

_____

_____

_____

_____

_____

You've written your own self-help essay on stress management. Keep it for future study. Feel free to pick another Bozo at a later time and write another essay.

CHAPTER 16

Seeking Mercy Instead of Justice

"Bless those who persecute you, bless and do not curse them." (Rom 12:14)

We've all seen the grizzly real-life courtroom dramas on the news—the parents of the murder victim weeping as the guilty verdict is read, having finally received "justice" and achieved "closure."

They may have received "justice" of a sort, but there is no "closure" on a dead child, and these parents' hearts still will not be at peace.

To achieve the peace that passes all human understanding, they are going to have to forgive their child's murderer—just as Christ asked the Father to forgive his killers even as he hung on the cross!

Here Christ calls us to the highest standard of human behavior; as always, he does so for our own sakes, for the sake of our very souls. We are to love our enemies: not tolerate, not abide, but love! And we are to love them not out of pious duty or because it's the law, but *because God loves them*.

Everyone we meet is a beloved son or daughter of God; everyone we meet is our sister or our brother.

We probably all harbor grudges in what one minister referred to as our "Hall of Hurts." Nurturing those ancient wrongs does nothing to the person who inflicted the hurt, but it may erode your faith and corrode your spirit.

Letting go is so hard—and so necessary.

See if you can bring to mind one of those hurts now. It may be as recent as today, or it may have been festering for decades. You may have many injuries to choose from. Select one and describe exactly what happened, just as you remember it.

A visit to the "Hall of Hurts"

_____

_____

_____

_____

_____

_____

_____

_____

_____

_____

_____

_____

_____

_____

_____

_____

_____

_____

_____

_____

_____

_____

_____

Put this essay aside for a day or more. Without rereading it yet, write about the same incident *from the point of view of the one who hurt you*. How might this person recount the event?

A side trip to the other person's point of view

_____

_____

_____

_____

_____

_____

_____

_____

_____

_____

_____

_____

_____

_____

This exercise may have been difficult, perhaps even painful, but I'm hoping it was also useful and illuminating.

Hold the offender up to our heavenly Father and ask God to forgive him or her, to nurture and care for and save that person. Continue to pray for that person's well-being (not that they "learn their lesson" or are sorry for what they did!).

This is the steep, narrow road to peace.

CHAPTER 17

Accepting the Inevitable

"The LORD will keep you from all evil; he will keep your life.
The LORD will keep your going out and your coming in
from this time on and forevermore." (Ps 121:7–8)

*O*n the last exercise, you toured your personal "Hall of Hurts," freeing one of the captives from your resentment and anger. Now I offer you the opportunity to take another unhappy walk down memory lane, this time looking for a time in your life when you faced serious challenges and were powerless to help yourself.

When I was crippled with rheumatoid arthritis and rheumatic fever at age eleven, there wasn't a whole lot I could do about it. Mostly, I just had to live with pain for long months of confinement.

I depended on my parents for all my needs, on my doctor for my medical care, and on all three for encouragement. I couldn't have asked for a better trio on all counts. I, in turn, attempted to be a "brave little soldier" for them.

I relied on God to deliver me from the horrid disease and, even more fundamentally, to be with me in my pain, fear, and struggle.

When I was sixteen or seventeen, a friend and I got caught in a riptide while bodysurfing off Newport Beach in Southern California. Fortunately, we knew what to do. Basically, what you do is nothing. A riptide is like quicksand. Struggling against it only makes it worse. You have to let it carry you out, away from shore, until you're outside its range and don't have to struggle so hard just to stay afloat. Then you wait for the rescue boat.

That boat came, thank God, and my companion and I were fine. Had we tried to swim against the killer tide, we may have drowned.

One more example again finds me attempting to bodysurf. (You'd think I would have learned my lesson!) An undercurrent took me under, ramming me hard against the sea bottom and knocking me senseless. I literally didn't know which way was up. Thrash and struggle as I might, I couldn't be sure I was even heading in the right direction. With my lungs begging for air and my head pounding, I finally went limp—and rose to the surface—to live another day and make more foolish mistakes.

At such times, we truly come to understand how much we rely on God's grace for our very breath. Life is a gift: there are no "self-made men or women." We really must "let go and let God."

Now, it's your turn. Spend some time now recalling three events from your life during which you had little or no control over your destiny. They may be life-and-death situations, but they don't have to be. They just have to be important to you. Describe each in a paragraph or two, as I have done here.

Three occasions when I realized how totally I rely on God

CHAPTER 18

Surrendering to Fear and Faith

"And remember, I am with you always, to the end of the age." (Mt 28:20)

On this chapter from *How to Handle Worry*, I revisited a fierce Arizona lightning storm and the savage down thrust of a Wisconsin tornado, occasions when I witnessed a hint of God's awesome power.

I might also have written about the serenity of Upper Clear Lake in the Gallatin Range of the Rocky Mountains, where I felt the presence of the Father and of my earthly father, recently deceased, dwelling in me.

God is with us at all times and in all places. Sometimes we're just more aware of him. It's almost as if God lets us catch a glimpse before he ducks back behind the curtain of creation until that time when we shall see him face-to-face.

Recall such a time in your life—a revelation, a God-moment—when you were more fully aware of the presence of God. Write about it here.

A God-moment

_____

_____

_____

_____

_____

_____

_____

_____

_____

_____

_____

_____

_____

Revisit your God-moments whenever you feel separated from him. Rest in the assurance that he is "with you always, until the end of the age."

As you worked through these exercises, teaching yourself how to use your faith to help you handle your worries, I hope you discovered how helpful it can be to write out your thoughts and prayers. Write about other God-moments from time to time, and keep a faith journal of your journey.

This work isn't finished. It's an ongoing process, the work of a lifetime, just as is our yearning to become ever closer to God. Go back to these exercises when you want and need to. Continue to explore Sacred Scripture and to pray always to your loving Father.

I will pray for you, and I ask you to keep me in your prayers as well. Remember that all things are possible with God, and that God loves you more than you can know.

Bibliography

Books that directly fed this book:

Bennett, Arnold. *How to Live on 24 Hours a Day*. New York: Doubleday, 1910.

Bennett, Hal Zina, and Susan Sparrow. *Follow Your Bliss*. New York: Avon Books (an imprint of HarperCollins Publishers), 1990.

Browne, Harry. *How I Found Freedom in an Unfree World*. London, UK: Macmillan, 1973.

Burns, David D. *Feeling Good: The New Mood Therapy*. New York: William Morrow (an imprint of HarperCollins Publishers), 1980.

Bolles, Richard Nelson. *The Three Boxes of Life—And How to Get Out of Them*. Berkeley, CA: Ten Speed Press, 1981.

Cousins, Norman. *The Healing Heart: Antidotes to Panic and Helplessness*. New York: W. W. Norton & Co., 1983.

Covey, Stephen R. *The 7 Habits of Highly Effective People*. New York: Fireside, Simon & Schuster, 1989.

Fanning, Tony and Robbie. *Get It All Done and Still Be Human*. Philadelphia: Chilton Book Company, 1979.

Franck, Frederick. *The Zen of Seeing*. New York: Vintage (a division of Random House), 1973.

Goulding, Mary McClure and Robert L. *Not to Worry*. New York: Silver Arrow/William Morrow, 1989.

Hauri, Peter, and Shirley Linde. *No More Sleepless Nights*. Hoboken, NJ: John Wiley & Sons, 1990.

Jones, Chuck. *Chuck Amuck: The Life and Times of an Animated Cartoonist*. New York: Farrar, Straus & Giroux, 1989.

Keyes, Ralph. *Timelock: How Life Got So Hectic and What You Can Do About It*. New York: HarperCollins, 1991.

Koestler, Arthur. *The Act of Creation*. London, UK: Macmillan, 1964.

Lakein, Alan. *How to Get Control of Your Time and Your Life*. New York: New American Library (an imprint of Penguin), 1973.

Lewis, C. S. *A Grief Observed*. San Francisco: Harper/San Francisco and Zondervan, 1996 (1961).

————. *Reflections on the Psalms*. New York: Harvest/Harcourt Brace, 1986 (1958).

————. *The Problem of Pain*. San Francisco: Harper/San Francisco, 1996 (1940).

Lindbergh, Anne Morrow. *A Gift from the Sea*. New York: Vintage (a division of Random House), 1991 (1955).

Linder, Staffan Burenstam. *The Harried Leisure Class*. New York: Columbia University Press, 1970.

Mackenzie, Alec. *The Time Trap*. New York: AMACON, 1990 (1972).

Nelson, John. *The Little Way of Saint Therese of Lisieux*. Liguori, MO: Liguori, 1997.

Oates, Wayne. *Confessions of a Workaholic*. New York: World Publishing/Times Mirror, 1971.

Pelletier, Kenneth R. *Healthy People in Unhealthy Places: Stress and Fitness at Work*. New York: Delacorte Press (a division of Random House), 1984.

Pelletier, Kenneth R. *Mind as Healer, Mind as Slayer*. New York: Delacorte Press (a division of Random House), 1977.

Prather, Hugh. *Notes on How to Live in the World...and Still Be Happy*. New York: Doubleday, 1986.

Schor, Juliet B. *The Overworked American: The Unexpected Decline of Leisure*. New York: Basic Books, 1991.

Schumacher, E. F. *Good Work*. New York: Harper & Row, 1979.

Sheehy, Gail. *Passages: Predictable Crises of Adult Life*. New York: Dutton (an imprint of Penguin), 1976.

Sinetar, Marsha. *Do What You Love, the Money Will Follow*. Mahwah, NJ: Paulist Press, 1987.

Smith, David, with Franklin Russell. *Healing Journey: The Odyssey of an Uncommon Athlete*. San Francisco: Sierra Club Books, 1983.

Smith, Donald G. *How to Cure Yourself of Positive Thinking*. Miami: E. A. Seemann Publishing, 1976.

Vaillant, George E. *Adaptation to Life*. Boston: Little, Brown, 1977.

Watts, Alan. *The Wisdom of Insecurity*. New York: Pantheon, 1951.

The Scripture quotations contained herein are from the *New Revised Standard Version Bible: Catholic Edition*, copyright © 1989, 1993, Division of Christian Education of the National Council of the Churches of Christ in the United States of America. Used by permission. All rights reserved.

Vatican II Weekday Missal. Boston: Pauline Books & Media, 2002.

My previous books on time and stress management include:

Cook, Marshall J. *Slow Down and Get More Done*. Cincinnati, OH: Betterway, 1993.

————. *Streetwise Time Management*. Avon, MA: Adams Media, 1999.

————. *Time Management: Proven Techniques for Making the Most of Your Valuable Time*. Avon, MA: Adams Media, 1998.

I won't attempt to list the poets and fiction writers who have shaped me. The list would be too long and the selections too subjective to be of much use here

auline
BOOKS & MEDIA

The Daughters of St. Paul operate book and media centers at the following addresses. Visit, call or write the one nearest you today, or find us on the World Wide Web, www.pauline.org

CALIFORNIA

3908 Sepulveda Blvd, Culver City, CA 90230	310-397-8676
2460 Broadway Street, Redwood City, CA 94063	650-369-4230
5945 Balboa Avenue, San Diego, CA 92111	858-565-9181

FLORIDA

145 S.W. 107th Avenue, Miami, FL 33174	305-559-6715

HAWAII

1143 Bishop Street, Honolulu, HI 96813	808-521-2731
Neighbor Islands call:	866-521-2731

ILLINOIS

172 North Michigan Avenue, Chicago, IL 60601	312-346-4228

LOUISIANA

4403 Veterans Memorial Blvd, Metairie, LA 70006	504-887-7631

MASSACHUSETTS

885 Providence Hwy, Dedham, MA 02026	781-326-5385

MISSOURI

9804 Watson Road, St. Louis, MO 63126	314-965-3512

NEW JERSEY

561 U.S. Route 1, Wick Plaza, Edison, NJ 08817	732-572-1200

NEW YORK

150 East 52nd Street, New York, NY 10022	212-754-1110

PENNSYLVANIA

9171-A Roosevelt Blvd, Philadelphia, PA 19114	215-676-9494

SOUTH CAROLINA

243 King Street, Charleston, SC 29401	843-577-0175

TENNESSEE

4811 Poplar Avenue, Memphis, TN 38117	901-761-2987

TEXAS

114 Main Plaza, San Antonio, TX 78205	210-224-8101

VIRGINIA

1025 King Street, Alexandria, VA 22314	703-549-3806

CANADA

3022 Dufferin Street, Toronto, ON M6B 3T5	416-781-9131

¡También somos su fuente para libros,
videos y música en español!